Fireflies

Written by Lucy Floyd

Celebration Press
Parsippany, New Jersey

Lights dance in the summer sky.
What are they? Fireflies!

Another name for this little insect is lightning bug.

Male fireflies blink in mid-air.

Female fireflies blink on leaves.

Fireflies use their lights to send messages to each other.

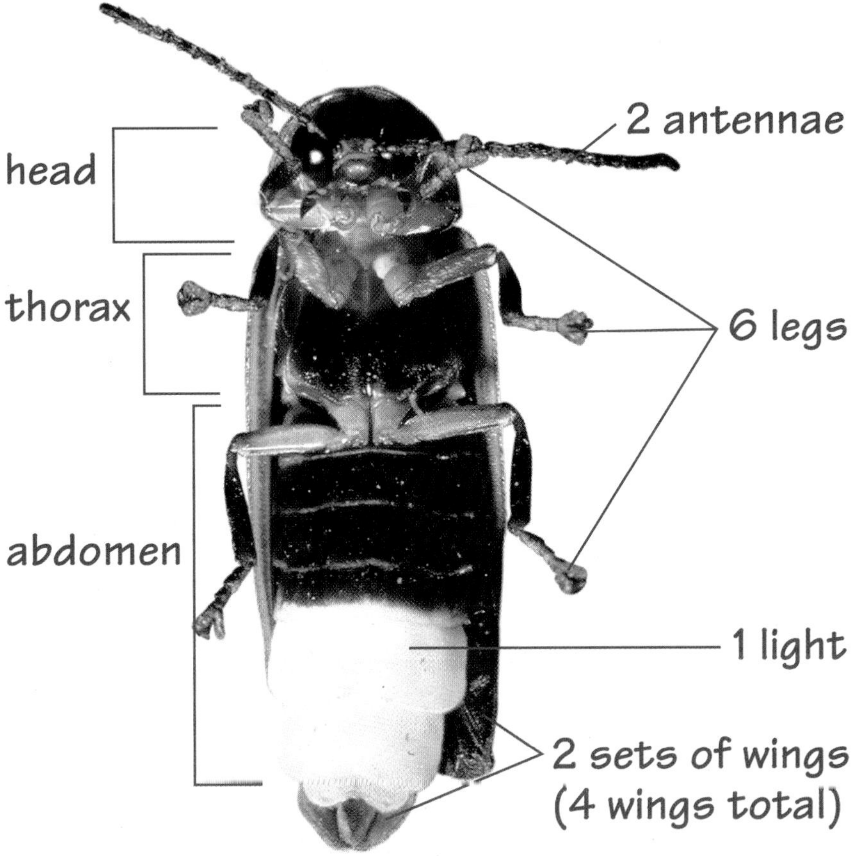

Like all insects, they have six legs.

Firefly Eggs

Firefly Larva

Female fireflies lay eggs.
A larva hatches from the egg.
A larva is a baby firefly.
The larva turns into a pupa.

Firefly Pupa

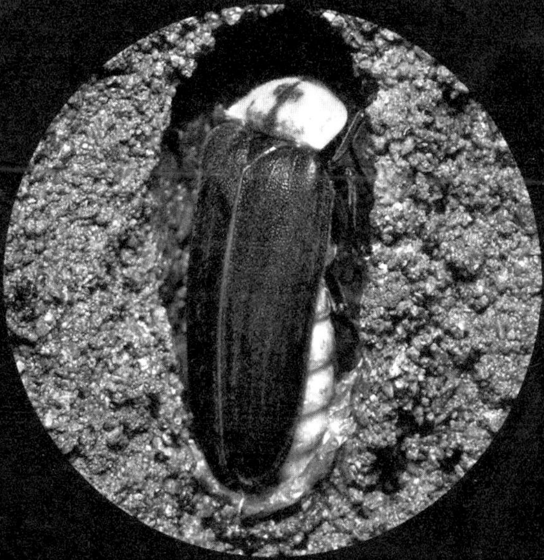

Adult Firefly

The pupa turns into an adult firefly.
It takes about two years for an egg to grow into a firefly!

Lights dance in the summer sky.
Fireflies!